BEAUTIFUL WOMEN WHO HAVE INFLUENCED HUMANITY

Island Of Beautiful Women

Culpepper Jill

VIRGINIA HALL

BACKGROUND

During World War II, Virginia Hall Goillot served in France with the secretive Special Operations Executive of the United Kingdom and the American Office of Strategic Services.

Barbara Virginia Hammel and Edwin Lee Hall gave birth to her on April 6, 1906, in Baltimore, Maryland. She studied French, Italian, and German at Roland Park Country School, Radcliffe College, and Barnard College. Virginia Hall studied French and Economics at George Washington University as well. She desired to complete her education in Europe, so she visited the continent and studied in France, Germany, and Austria before getting a job as a Consular Service clerk at the American Embassy in Warsaw, Poland, in 1931. Her mother's middle name was Virginia. As a child, she attended Roland Park Country School, an all-girls prep school. She went on to Radcliffe College and subsequently Barnard College, both prominent women's colleges, where she studied French, German, and Italian. Hall moved to Europe to finish her studies with her parents' backing. In the late 1920s, she travelled widely across Europe, studying in Austria, France, and Germany to join the diplomatic corps.

Her father owned a cinema in Baltimore, and she was a modern language aficionado who mastered German, French, and Italian. In 1950, on July 8, she married Paul Goillot, an 'Office of Strategic Services agent.

Virginia started working as a clerk for the Consular Service at the American embassy in Warsaw, Poland, in 1931 to progress to a full-fledged Foreign Service career. She was, however, asked to join friends on a hunting expedition while serving at the American embassy in Turkey in 1932. Her gun unexpectedly discharged during the journey and when they were in a secluded place. The bullet struck hall's left foot. The affected leg had to be amputated to survive when her companions transported her to the hospital.

Her usual diplomatic career was cut short when she was forced to adapt to life with a wooden limb she called "Cuthbert." In 1939, Hall resigned from the State Department and returned to Washington, D.C., to attend American University's graduate program.

Despite her best efforts to keep the incident from deterring her, it put a stumbling block in her way to pursuing her dream of working in the Foreign Service. She had to leave her job in 1939 because a U.S. State Department law prohibited anyone's amputation of a portion of a limp from working.

She returned to the United States, frustrated and tired of being rejected and limited, and had a wooden limb made for her. She began exercising to be able to do practically everything she could before. She was limping and couldn't run as fast as she used to. Aside from that, she was a natural leader who could handle herself. She returned to Europe, but she realized she would have to change her goals. The State Department would reject someone with a prosthetic limb.

Hall repeatedly tried to join the US Foreign Service as a diplomat, but the department rarely hired women. The Department of State turned her down in 1937 due to a rule prohibiting the hiring of disabled people as diplomats. Even a request to President Franklin D. Roosevelt, who was also crippled, went unheeded for her to be recruited. In March 1939, she resigned from the Department of State as a consular clerk. After working at many American embassies, she got keen to work for the US State Department. She aspired to be a member of the diplomatic corps. She aspired to be a member of the diplomatic corps.

Hall was in Paris when World War II broke out in Europe in 1940, having joined the Ambulance Service to aid in the war effort in France, but she ended up in Vichy territory when France fell to the invading Nazis. Hall was able to leave France and travel to London, where she joined the Special Operations Executive, a British intelligence outfit, as a volunteer.

The British 'Special Operations Executive' recruited Virginia as a special agent in 1941. In August of that year, she returned to France under the guise of a 'New York Post' correspondent, using the codename "Mary." For the next fifteen months, she helped develop a defiance network in Vichy.

Hall spent over a year in Vichy, France, trying to coordinate the activities of the French Resistance under the guise of a reporter for the New York Post. Hall went undercover as a journalist after only a few weeks with the SOE. She relocated to a Nazi-occupied region of France in the south. Virginia Hall worked hard to establish secure drop zones for Allies; this allowed for the introduction of new agents, supplies, money, and weaponry. In 1942, she worked on a handful of missions with Peter Churchill, a well-known SOE operative, involving the transportation of money and agents to French intelligence networks. Following that, Hall generally worked in and around Toulouse and Lyon.

She worked hard after coming to Lyons in 1942, but when the Germans unexpectedly captured France in November 1942, their suspicions of her rose, and she fled to Spain. After that, she worked in Madrid for the British 'Special Operations Executive' (SOE). After returning to London in July 1943, she was made an honorary 'Member of the Order of the British Empire.'

In March 1944, she joined the 'Special Operations Branch' of the US Office of Strategic Services and was transferred back to France on March 21. She was landed on the Brittany Coast by a British MTB since her "Cuthbert" hindered her from using a parachute. This time she entered France under the guise of Marcelle Montagne, while her associates referred to her as "Daine."

Hall got married to Goillot; they both worked for the CIA, where Hall worked as an intelligence analyst focusing on French parliamentary issues. Hall and Goillot were assigned to the CIA's Special Activities Division, specializing in covert operations.

After fifteen years, Hall left the CIA in 1966 and moved to Barnesville, Maryland, with her husband. She died in 1982 in Rockville, Maryland, and was buried in the 'Druid Ridge Cemetery in Pikesville, Maryland.

A BEAUTIFUL PERFECT SPY'S ADVENTURE

Virginia Hall was a well-known spy who helped the French Resistance during WWII, working for British and American intelligence and becoming one of the Nazis' most sought adversaries.

During World War II, Hall worked in France with the secretive Special Operations Executive of the United Kingdom and the American Office of Strategic Services. The mission of SOE and OSS in occupied Europe was to perform espionage, sabotage, and surveillance against the Axis forces, particularly Nazi Germany. SOE and OSS agents formed alliances with resistance groups in France and provided them with guns and equipment dropped from England. Following WWII, Hall worked for the Central Intelligence Agency's Special Activities Division.

Hall was one of the founding agents for the SOE and the first female agent to settle in France. In Lyon, she founded the Heckler network. She "became an expert at support operations, organizing resistance movements, supplying agents with money, weapons, and supplies, assisting downed airmen in escaping, and offering safe homes and medical treatment to wounded agents and pilots" over the next 15 months.

When the SOE heard that the German Gestapo was coming toward southern France, the SOE urged the resistance organizers to clear out of Lyon, and she had to flee France in November 1942 to avoid capture by the Germans. Hall boarded a train with the rest of the gang. The escape was difficult, as it included a 30-mile excursion that had to be completed on foot. The guide who consented to accompany them was irritated by the presence of a woman. As a result, Hall did everything she could to hide her limp. It had been a long journey.

The party made it back to London, where they began training to use wireless radio to communicate. They were well aware that communication was crucial.

She returned to France in 1944 as a wireless operator for the OSS and a member of the Saint network, where she supplied arms, training, and direction to French resistance groups, especially in Haute-Loire, where the Maquis cleared the department of German soldiers before the arrival of the American army in September 1944.

By this time, the Germans had discovered that a woman is known as La Dame Qui Boite, or the Limping Lady, was one of the main organizers. They gave orders to track her down and apprehend her. After completing her training, Virginia Hall moved to join the Office of Strategic Services, an American intelligence outfit.

She was sent back to France for more covert work on this assignment. This time she pretended to be an elderly farmer. Her uneven walk was better concealed by the bulky garments in conjunction with her aged outfit.

She worked as a cowgirl and lived with a farmer's family. She also went to a nearby market to sell the farmer's cheese and milk. She frequently overheard German officers conversing there.

She would pull out her radio as soon as she returned to the farm and wired in whatever information she gathered. Hall and her squad damaged bridges, railways, and telephone lines while undercover, killing over 150 Germans and capturing over 500.

As a World War II secret agent, Hall had to learn the "exacting chores of being available, arranging contacts, recommending who to bribe and where to hide, soothing the raw nerves of agents on the run, and coordinating the distribution of radio equipment" on her own.

Jean Rousset, a gynecologist, and Germaine Guérin, the owner of a major brothel in Lyon, were among her recruiters. Guérin made multiple safe homes available to Hall and relayed the information she and her female employees received from German officers visiting the brothel.

The Germans nicknamed Virginia Hall "Artemis', and the Gestapo reportedly thought of her as "the most dangerous of all Allied spies, Lady with Limp, the attractive deadly enemy spy who observes and exposes their activities and plans."

Some of the world's most distinguished distinctions have been awarded to Hall. She also won a Distinguished Service Cross from the American government, the first such decoration bestowed to a woman during World War II.

In the meantime, the French honored her with the Croix de Guerre for her service in occupied France. The honors continued after her death: she was honored by the French and British ambassadors to the United States in 2006 on what would have been her 100th birthday, and she was inducted into the Maryland Women's Hall of Fame in 2019.

She is, to date, remembered as one of the most successful and well-respected spies in American history.

<u>CONTRIBUTIONS AND INFLUENCE OF VIRGINIA HALL IN WORLD WAR II</u>

Virginia had always been known as a young lady who loved adventure. "Capricious and cantankerous," she described herself. She likes going on hunts. She once wore a bracelet made of live snakes to school. This spirit provided the foundation for perseverance and continued participation in World War II, helping the government to have a profound influence.

Hall volunteered to operate an ambulance for the French when the Nazis invaded France during WWII. On the other hand, France was quickly overrun, compelling her to flee to the United Kingdom. She was introduced to British intelligence after an accidental meeting with a spy.

After receiving scant training, she was among the first British spies dispatched into Nazi-occupied France in 1941. Hall was a natural spy, always one step ahead of the "Gestapo," the German secret police. She was able to take advantage of the Gestapo's chauvinism at the time, as no one in Germany believed a woman could be a spy early in the war.

Hall was based in Lyon, a city in eastern France. She resided in a monastery and enlisted the aid of the nuns. She subsequently contacted a female brothel owner and learned that German forces had obtained intelligence from French prostitutes.

The Germans realized they needed to pursue a limping woman who had become a significant threat to their mission. Despite the 'Gestapo's high alert, she managed to tell the Allies of the Germans' move of headquarters from Lyons to Le Puy.

However, as the Gestapo's hunt for her intensified, she was forced to flee to the Haute-Loire region to join the 'French Resistance.' Hall coordinated French resistance fighters and provided a haven for them.

According to Hall, the 12 operatives detained by French police in October 1941 were jailed at the Mauzac prison near Bergerac.

Georges Bégué, a wireless operator, smuggled messages to Hall from the prison, and she enlisted the help of Gaby Bloch, the wife of one of the inmates, to plot an escape. Bloch visited the prison regularly to bring her husband food and other supplies, including tins of sardines.

Bégué could fabricate a key to the barracks' door where the inmates were held using the tools she sneaked in and the sardine tins. Hall gathered safe homes, vehicles, and extra hands. A priest snuck a radio inside Bégué, and he began transmitting to London from inside the prison.

The inmates escaped on July 15, 1942, with the help of Virginia Hall and took refuge in the woods while the French police searched. The escape was dubbed "one of the most useful operations of its sort" throughout the war.

The American Consulate in Lyon informed Hall on November 7, 1942, that an allied invasion of North Africa was impending. On November 8, in reaction to the invasion, the Germans advanced into Vichy, France. Hall rightly predicted that the Gestapo and Abwehr would intensify their suppression. When the Nazis closed in on her near the end of 1942, she fled Lyon without notifying anyone, going on a terrible trek that included walking 50 miles in deep snow over the rugged Pyrenees Mountains.

In 1944 and 1945, Virginia Hall's second operation in France was considerably more effective than the first.

Her network numbered around 1,500 people, including Paul Goillot, a French-American soldier who subsequently became her husband. She ordered airdrops for the rebel fighters, who detonated bombs on bridges and derailed trains. She also regained villages long before Allied forces marched deep into France.

Hall travelled around France south of Paris from March to July 1944. She arranged multiple safe houses, discovered and organized drop zones, and developed and restored relationships with the Resistance, particularly Philippe de Vomecourt. She formed multiple resistance cells in the Cher and Cosne , each with a hundred men, and provided them; she also laid out drop zones where she could transfer commandos, money, guns, and other supplies from England.

When the Allied Forces disembarked in Normandy, she set up safe shelters. She tried unsuccessfully to plan a jailbreak to release three German prisoners she referred to as her nephews. She worked with SOE in Madrid for a while before returning to London in July 1943; she became a distinguished member of the Order of the British Empire.

Another major influence and effort during WWII were assisting British airmen who had been shot down or crashed over Europe in escaping and returning to England.

Downed airmen who arrived in Lyon were told to go to the American Consulate and ask for "Olivier," one of her codenames. She concealed, nourished, and assisted hundreds of airmen to flee France to neutral Spain and then back to England with the help of brothel owner Guerin and other associates.

Following that, Hall assisted the Maquis in southern France in harassing the Germans in preparation for the invasion of the south, Operation Dragoon, on August 15, 1944. In July, Hall was assigned to the Haute-Loire department, where she arrived on July 14, dropped her disguise, and set up shop in a barn near Le Chambon-Sur-Lignon.

The three Maquisard battalions in her region carried out a series of effective sabotage operations, forcing the German occupants to flee Le Puy-en-Velay and join the rest of the retreating German soldiers heading north.

In April 1945, Hall and Golliot returned to Paris after she and her battalions had defeated the Nazis. She resigned from OSS after writing reports and identifying those who had aided her and deserved commendations.

Right after the war, Hall returned to Lyon to learn what had happened to the people who had worked for and assisted her there. Her closest associates, brothel owner Germaine Guérin and doctor Jean Rousset were both caught by the Germans and sent to prison camps, but they managed to escape. Guérin received 80,000 francs in compensation from the United Kingdom, which she arranged.

In September 1945, General William Joseph Donovan personally presented her with the Distinguished Service Cross, the only one to be awarded to a civilian woman during World War II, recognizing her actions in France.

Virginia Hall did not leave a memoir, did not accept interviews, and spoke little about her time abroad, even with family. She is, to date, the only civilian woman to receive the American Distinguished Service Cross during WWII. She turned down all but a private ceremony with OSS chief Donovan and a presentation by President Truman. She is remembered and respected as one of the most effective and revered spies who fought and served in World War II, favorably benefiting humanity.

MARIE CURIE

BACKGROUND AND EARLY LIFE

On November 7, 1867, Maria Sklodowska, who later became known as Marie Curie, was born in the Warsaw Congress Kingdom of Poland, the Russian Empire. She was a polish-born French scientist who is most known for her work on radioactivity has won the Nobel Prize twice.

She was the last of four siblings, having three older sisters and a brother.

Maria's older siblings were Zofia, who was born in 1862 and was nicknamed Zosia; Józef, who was born in 1863 and was nicknamed Józio; Bronisawa, who was born in 1865 and was nicknamed Bronia, Helena, who was born in 1866 and was nicknamed Hela, and Marie, nicknamed Mania, was the youngest of five children born to Wladyslaw, her father, and Bronis. Curie's father was a math and physics teacher, and her mother, who died when she was 11 years old, was also a teacher.

Curie inherited her father's traits as a child. She had an exceptionally sharp and curious mind, excelled in school, and was known for her incredible recall. Despite being a star student in high school, Curie was denied admission to the male-only University of Warsaw due to gender bias in Poland's educational system. However, she completed her studies in Warsaw's "floating university," which consisted of a series of hidden, underground classes.

Maria began attending J. Sikorska's boarding school when she was eleven years old; after that, she attended a gymnasium for females, where she graduated with a gold medal on June 12, 1883.Her older sister Zofia became ill and died of typhus when she was ten years old, and her mother died of tuberculosis two years later.

Marie had a terrible period as her father, a math and physics teacher, lost his assets due to a bad investment. Wladyslaw Skodowski also served as the director of two boys' gymnasia in Warsaw. He was subsequently sacked by his Russian supervisors for pro-Polish sympathies and forced to seek lower-paying jobs; the family also lost money on a faulty investment and eventually decided to augment their income by lodging boys in the house after Russian authorities withdrew laboratory instruction from Polish schools.

Furthermore, the family had also lost property and fortunes in both the paternal and maternal families due to patriotic participation in Polish national uprisings to regain Poland's independence. Józef Skodowski, Maria's biological grandpa, was the principal of the Lublin elementary school where Boleslaw Prus, a significant figure in Polish literature, attended.

The ensuing generation, including Maria and her older siblings, were condemned to struggle to make ends meet. As a result, she worked as a teacher while secretly participating in the nationalist "free university," reading in Polish to female employees.

She received a gold medal for completing her secondary education at the Russian lycée at 16 due to her extraordinary memory and brightness. Marie intended to go to university after graduating from high school, but this was not something young ladies in Poland did in the 1800s. The university was exclusively for men. However, women were allowed to attend the Sorbonne, a prestigious university in Paris, France.

Marie was passionate about education and wanted to attend Sorbonne University in Paris. Still, there were no financial means to make this possible, and her father could not support her.

Curie and her sister Bronya wanted to study abroad and get a formal degree, but their family was not financially buoyant enough to achieve this.

Curie was determined, and she struck a pact with her sister to work and earn enough money to fund and pay for her sister's medical school education in exchange for Bronya returning the favour after she finished her studies. Curie became a nanny at the age of 17 to assist pay for her sister's attendance at medical school in Paris. Curie was able to fund her sister Bronisawa's medical studies in Paris with her wages, and she continued to study on her own. Curie worked as a governess and tutor for about five years. She spent her free time studying physics, chemistry, and mathematics.

A few months before, Bronislawa, who had married Kazimierz Duski, a Polish physician and social and political leader, invited Maria to join them in Paris at the beginning of 1890. On the other hand, Maria had to decline because she couldn't afford the travel expenses and University tuition, which would take her another year and a half to save up for.

Curie, however, obtained a job as a governess at the age of 18 to ensure that she did not forfeit the opportunity for higher education. Her father stepped in to assist her, and he was able to arrange a more profitable position for her.

She continued to educate herself throughout this time by reading books, exchanging letters, and tutoring herself. She worked as a governess until late 1891. She also tutored and began her practical scientific studies in a chemical laboratory at Warsaw's Museum of Industry and Agriculture, Krakowskie Przedmiecie, her cousin Józef Boguski, who had worked as an assistant to Russian chemist Dmitri Mendeleev in Saint Petersburg, ran the laboratory.

Curie ultimately made it to Paris in 1891, set off for Paris in November and enrolled at the Sorbonne. She enrolled at the Sorbonne University in Paris, where she studied physics and mathematics, having developed a genuine interest in the sciences due to her voracious desire to study. Curie signed her name as "Marie" when she registered at the Sorbonne in Paris to appear more French.

She stayed with her sister and her husband for a short time in Paris before renting a garret in the Latin Quarter closer to the university and studying chemistry, physics and mathematics at the University of Paris.

Curie was a focused and devoted student who immersed herself in her studies. This commitment came at a personal cost: Curie survived on buttered bread and tea since she had no money, and her health suffered due to her poor diet, yet she was still at the top of her class.

She survived on what she had, keeping herself warm during the frigid winters by wearing everything she owned. She was so concentrated on her studies that she occasionally forgot to eat. Sklodowska studied throughout the day and tutored in the evenings to make ends meet. She received a physics degree in 1893 and began working in Gabriel Lippmann's industrial laboratory.

The Alexandrovitch Scholarship for Polish citizens studying abroad was given to her in honor of her talents.

Curie resumed her studies at the University of Paris, where she accomplished her master's degree in physics in 1893. Afterward, she got another degree in mathematics the following year, 1893, with the help of a fellowship. Marie Sklodowska began her scientific career in Paris, where the Society commissioned her to investigate the magnetic properties of various steels.

Pierre Curie, a French scientist, entered her life the same year; they were drawn together by their shared passion for natural sciences.

Pierre Curie was a professor at the Higher Educational Institution for Industrial Physics and Chemistry in the City of Paris (ESPCI Paris). They were introduced by a colleague, Polish physicist Józef Wierusz-Kowalski, who had learned that Marie needed more lab space, which Wierusz-Kowalski knew Pierre could provide.

Marie, after graduating from Sorbonne University; Marie had been commissioned to research various types of steel and its magnetic properties, and she needed a lab to conduct her research. Although Pierre did not have a huge laboratory, he located some room for her to begin working.

Soon after, the smart team established a romantic relationship, and they evolved into a dynamic scientific duo who was entirely devoted to one another.

Marie married French physicist Pierre Curie in Sceaux on July 26, 1895; neither desired a religious ceremony; Curie wore a dark blue gown, which she wore instead of a wedding gown.

They had two common interests: lengthy bicycle rides and honeymoon excursions overseas, which brought them closer together.

Marie had found a partner, love, and scientific collaborator in Pierre, and she could count on him. Marie and Pierre initially worked on separate projects. On the other hand, Pierre put aside his work to assist Marie with her studies after she discovered radioactivity.

The Curies lacked a permanent laboratory, so they conducted most of their research in a converted shed close to ESPCI. The hut, which had previously served as a dissecting facility for medical students, was inadequately ventilated and not even watertight. They were completely oblivious to the harmful repercussions of radiation exposure that came with their continued unprotected work with radioactive materials.

ESPCI did not fund her research, but she did receive funding from metallurgical and mining businesses and other organizations and governments.

In 1897, Marie and Pierre welcomed their first child, Irène. In 1904, the couple welcomed their second child, Eve. However, in 1903, Marie and Pierre lost a child who was delivered prematurely, just before the birth of their second daughter. Though the Curies were unaware of it, radiation poisoning from dealing with radioactive material had begun to take its toll, resulting in stillbirth.

Marie's scientific career was not disrupted by the births of her two daughters, Irène and Louise, in 1897 and 1904. Curie began teaching lecturing at the École Normale Supérieure to support her family and became a lecturer in physics at the École Normale Supérieure for Girls in Sèvres, where she created an experimental demonstration-based teaching technique. In December 1904, she was promoted to chief assistant in Pierre Curie's laboratory.

Marie Sklodowska Curie, who went by both surnames, never lost touch with her Polish roots while a French citizen. She educated her girls in Polish and took them to Poland on vacations. Her first chemical element, polonium, was named after her home country.

On April 19, 1906, while going across the Rue Dauphine in severe rain, Pierre Curie was hit by a horse vehicle and fell under its wheels, his skull was fractured, and he died instantaneously. Marie Curie became a widowed mother to her two young girls due to this. The loss of Curie's husband had a profound effect on her.

On May 13, 1906, the University of Paris' physics department chose to keep the chair occupied by her late husband and offer it to Marie. She accepted it, hoping to build a world-class laboratory as a memorial to her late husband, Pierre.

Despite the catastrophe that had just struck her, her indomitable spirit kept her working, and she went on to follow in his step as a Professor at the Sorbonne and continue lecturing where he had left off.

She won a second Nobel Prize in 1911 for developing a method of measuring radioactivity. Soon after, Sorbonne established the first radium institution, which included two laboratories: one for radiation research directed by Marie Curie and the other for biological cancer research.

When World War I broke out, Marie discovered that doctors could utilize X-rays to figure out what was wrong with an injured soldier. However, there were insufficient X-ray machines to provide one to every hospital.

She proposed that the X-ray machines be transported by truck from one hospital to the next. Marie even assisted with the machine training. The trucks were dubbed "little Curies" for their assistance to over a million soldiers during the war.

Unfortunately, the harmful consequences of ionizing radiation were unknown at the time of her research, conducted without the safety precautions that future scientists would subsequently adopt. She kept test tubes carrying radioactive isotopes in her pocket and kept them in her desk drawer, marveling how faintly the substances emitted light in the dark. While serving as a radiologist at field hospitals during the war, Curie was exposed to X-rays from unprotected equipment.

Marie's work as a researcher, teacher, and laboratory director continued after the war. She received numerous accolades and prizes; Ellen Richards Research Prize, Grand Prix du Marquis d'Argenteuil (1923), and Edinburgh University's Cameron Prize. She received countless honorary degrees from universities around the world.

She died of aplastic anemia on July 4, 1934, at the age of 66, in the Sancellemoz sanatorium in Passy, Haute-Savoie, from long-term radiation exposure that damaged her bone marrow. She and her husband Pierre were buried together at the Sceaux cemetery. In 1995, both bones were relocated to the Panthéon in Paris sixty years later in honor of their achievements. Because of the radiation they had been exposed to when living, their corpses were enclosed inside a lead lining. She was the Panthéon's second female internment and the first woman to be honored with a place in the Panthéon solely for her achievements.

Marie Curie, during her lifetime, was a Polish and French physicist who researched radioactivity. Marie Curie made the record as the first female to win the Nobel Prize. She co-won her first Nobel Prize alongside her husband, Pierre Curie, making them the first couple to win the Nobel Prize and this established the Curie family legacy of having five distinct Nobel Prizes. In 1906, she became the first female to become a professor at the University of Paris.

One of Marie Curie's outstanding achievements was accumulating intense radioactive properties, proffer treatment to illness, and maintaining an abundant supply for research in nuclear physics.

MOTHER OF PHYSICS

Marie Curie's relentless resolve and insatiable curiosity made her an icon in the world of modern science. She discovered polonium and radium, sponsored the use of radiation in medicine, and fundamentally changed our understanding of radioactivity.

Marie Curie was the first famously known female scientist in the world. She was identified as the mother of Modern Physics for her research about radioactivity, which she coined.

The journey of becoming the mother of science began in 1895. Wilhelm Röntgen had discovered the existence of X-rays, though users did not yet understand the mechanism behind their production at the time. In 1896, Henri Becquerel discovered that uranium salts emitted rays that resembled X-rays in their penetrating power. That year, Curie decided to look into uranium rays as a possible field of research for a thesis. She recorded that an ore containing uranium was more radioactive than explained by its uranium content; this led to the discovery of an element that happened to be 400 times more radioactive than uranium. In 1898 science included it in the Periodic Table as polonium, named after Curie's birth country.

She began systematic research for additional substances that emit radiation, and by 1898 she was able to establish that the element thorium was more radioactive. Pierre Curie was fascinated by her discoveries. By mid-1898 got so involved that he had to drop his work on crystals and join her. She used a different technique to observe samples. Using her husband's electrometer, she concluded that uranium rays caused the air around a sample to conduct electricity. Her first conclusion was that the activity of the uranium compounds depended only on the quantity of uranium present. She developed a hypothesis that the radiation was not a result of molecules' interaction came from the atom. This hypothesis served as a crucial step in disproving the assumption that atoms were indivisible. The research idea was her own, as no one had assisted her in developing it, and she took it to her husband for assessment.

Many scientists found it difficult to accept that a female scientist could be capable of the original work in which she was part as a result of sexism in the Science sector had that time, which her achievement broke, at this early point of her career Curie and her husband presented a joint paper in July 1898 announcing the discovery of an element they named "polonium," after her native Poland.

The Curies announced the finding of a second element on December 26, 1898, which they dubbed "radium" from the Latin word "ray." They also invented the term "radioactivity" during their research, which has since become a well-known occurrence in physics.

Her former professor, Gabriel Lippmann, presented her with a paper to the Académie on April 12, 1898, offering a brief and straightforward summary of her work.

Unfortunately, just as Thompson had been defeated by Becquerel in the race to report her discovery that thorium emits rays just like uranium, Gerhard Carl Schmidt beat Curie in the race to report her discovery since Gerhard Carl Schmidt had published his findings two months earlier in Berlin.

During her investigation, Marie discovered that pitchblende samples, a mineral containing uranium ore, were far more radioactive than pure uranium. Further research convinced her that the extremely high readings she was getting were not due to uranium alone and that something else was present in the pitchblende. Because it had never been discovered before, it could only exist in trace amounts, and it appeared to be extremely radioactive. Marie was certain she had discovered a brand-new chemical element. Pierre and Marie Curie got to work looking for the elusive element.

They ground pitchblende samples, dissolved them in acid, and then used standard analytical chemical techniques to isolate the various elements. They eventually recovered polonium; a black substance that was 330 times more radioactive than uranium. Polonium, with the atomic number 84, was a brand-new chemical element.

When the Curies dug deeper, they discovered that the liquid left over after extracting the polonium was still radioactive. They discovered that pitchblende included a new element that was significantly more radioactive than polonium but only existed in trace amounts.

The Curies weighed a 100-gram sample of pitchblende and pulverized it using a pestle and mortar on April 14, 1898. They were not aware of it, but what they were looking for was present in such little amounts that they'd have to treat tons of ore to get it.

The Curies released substantial evidence indicating the presence of the new element radium in 1898, but they still didn't have a sample. Because pitchblende contains valuable uranium, it was a costly material, and Marie needed a lot of it.

She contacted an Austrian business that extracted the uranium from pitchblende for industrial use and purchased many tons of the worthless waste product, which was far more radioactive than the original pitchblende and was significantly cheaper. Marie began processing the pitchblende to remove the minuscule amounts of radium.

Grinding, dissolving, filtering, precipitating, collecting, redissolving, crystallizing, and recrystallizing were all done on a much greater scale than before, with 20kg batches of the material. The labor was strenuous, physically demanding, and exposed the Curies to hazards. They began to feel poorly and physically exhausted during this time, and their illness can now be traced to and compared to the early signs of radiation sickness. They persisted despite the dangers, frequently with raw and irritated hands from handling highly radioactive material daily.

Marie finally isolated radium as radium chloride in 1902 and determined its atomic weight to be 225.93. Although the route to the discovery was long and difficult, she was well aware of the need to publicize her findings as soon as possible to establish herself as a priority.

The Curies published 32 scientific articles between 1898 and 1902, including one that claimed that when malignant tumor-forming cells were exposed to radium, radium destroyed them faster than healthy cells.

Curie became the first woman member of the École Normale Supérieure in 1900, and her husband joined the University of Paris faculty the following year. At her father's death in 1902, she traveled to Poland.

On the other hand, Marie Curie has become a scientific icon, receiving homage from all around the world. Because the board members believed that women could not be members of the Institute of France, Marie Curie was not elected to the French Academy of Sciences by one vote early in 1911.

Marie Curie refused to allow the Academy to publish any of her work for the next ten years. The press attacked her nomination. Despite this, she was named director of the Marie Curie Laboratory, part of the University of Paris' Radium Institute, and the Institute for Radioactivity in Warsaw. She was awarded a second Nobel Prize in the same year.

She undertook the world's first studies into treating neoplasms with radioactive isotopes under her guidance. She established the Curie Institute in Paris in 1920 and the Curie Institute in Warsaw in 1932, both of which are prominent medical research centers today. She designed mobile radiography units to provide X-ray services to field hospitals treating wounded soldiers during World War I.

Marie Curie earned a name for herself in science, and we can find her name in every nook and cranny of the discipline.

In honor of her and Pierre Curie, the Curie (sign Ci) is a unit of radioactivity.

Curium is the name given to the element with the atomic number 96.

Curite, sklodowskite, and cuprosklodowskite are three radioactive minerals named after the Curies.

The European Union's Marie Sklodowska-Curie Actions fellowship program, which supports young scientists who want to work in other countries, is named after her.

Curie and Pierre were both honored in 2007 when a metro station in Paris was christened after them.

Maria is the name of a nuclear research reactor in Poland.

The asteroid 7000 Curie was named after Marie Curie.

The Curies went to work as researchers at the School of Chemistry and Physics in Paris, where they began their groundbreaking research on uranium's invisible rays.

In addition, Poland designated 2011 as Marie Curie's Year, and the United Nations designated it as the International Year of Chemistry.

MARIE CURIE'S CONTRIBUTIONS TO SCIENCE AND HUMANITY

Marie Curie, known as the "Mother of Science," made a reputation for herself. Still, she also made significant contributions to the expansion and existence of science as a field and humanity as a whole.

The Curies' work shaped the world of science in the twentieth and twenty-first centuries in both physical and societal aspects. Curie's work helped overturn conventional beliefs in physics and chemistry, but it also had a significant impact on society. She had to overcome hurdles erected in her native and adopted countries because she was a woman to achieve her scientific achievements.

The radiation of radium was so high that Curie couldn't ignore it. It went against the conservation of energy concept, forcing a rethinking of physics' underpinnings.

Curie's work helped to upset conventional beliefs in physics and chemistry, and it has had an equally profound impact in the sociological realm. She had to overcome hurdles erected in her native and adopted countries because she was a woman to achieve her scientific achievements.

Henri Becquerel's discovery of radioactivity in 1896 motivated the Curies in their revolutionary research and analysis that led to the isolation of polonium, called after Marie's native nation, and radium, which transformed the science world. Curie devised procedures for isolating radium from radioactive leftovers in large quantities to allow for its characterization and detailed examination of its qualities, including therapeutic properties.

Curie propounded the use of radium to eliminate suffering throughout her life, and during World War I, she devoted herself to this endeavor with the help of her daughter, Irene. She maintained her passion for science throughout her life and contributed significantly to establishing a radiation laboratory in her hometown.

In 1929, President Herbert Hoover of the United States gave her a $ 50,000 grant from American science friends to purchase radium for use in the Warsaw laboratory.

Radium and polonium were discovered and employed rapidly and uncontrollably in all aspects of life and medicine. However, the lack of suitable dosimetric procedures and safety precautions resulted in many serious problems. Marie Sklodowska-Curie had firsthand experience with this. Gaining experience with side effects led to creating contemporary radiation principles and safety measures. In today's oncology, radiation is a crucial therapeutic approach.

Curie recognized via observation and experiments that wounded aids best-served troops if they were operated on as quickly as possible during World War I. She identified the necessity for radiological field centers at the front lines of the battle to help battlefield surgeons avoid amputations when treatment may salvage limbs.

After studying radiology, anatomy, and automobile mechanics, she constructed X-ray equipment, vehicles, auxiliary generators, and mobile radiography units, known as Petites Curies or Little Curies. She rose through the Red Cross Radiology Service ranks and established France's first military radiology center, which opened in late 1914.

They operated at casualty clearing stations close to the front line, X-raying wounded men to find fractures, bullets, and shrapnel, initially aided by a military doctor and her 17-year-old daughter Irène. In the first year of the war, Curie oversaw the installation of 20 mobile radiological vehicles and another 200 radiological units on the field.

Although Wilhelm Roentgen discovered X-Rays in 1895, the X-Ray equipment used to treat the wounded had a restriction. They were only discovered in hospitals located far from the battleground. Petites Curie, or mobile radiological machines, were born due to her efforts. Curie built a dynamo in the mobile car to create and provide the required electricity to overcome the problem of providing electricity.

Marie Curie's technology is comparable to that used today in hospitals' fluoroscopy machines, which are sophisticated X-ray machines that allow doctors to view moving images in the body, such as the heart's pumping action or swallowing motion. Curie's study was crucial in the development of contemporary surgical x-rays.

She was named head of the International Red Cross's radiological service, and she taught medical workers and doctors about x-ray equipment operations and usage. She went on to train other women to work as aides.

Curie assisted doctors in locating and removing shrapnel and bullets from the bodies of wounded soldiers by equipping and operating more than twenty ambulances and hundreds of field hospitals with simple x-ray machines during the war.

She not only directly trained and supervised young women in the use of the equipment, but she also drove and operated one herself, despite the dangers of being so close to the front lines of battle.

She worked in a Casualty Clearing Station alongside her daughter Irene, where she assisted in detecting gunshots, fractured bones, and other interior injuries using X-Ray machines. She oversaw the installation of 20 mobile radiology vans and 200 radiology units at field hospitals in the first year of the war. She also trained around 150 women to work as X-Ray assistants.

Curie's x-ray equipment and the Radon gas syringes she invented to sterilize wounds were estimated to have saved a million soldiers by the war's end. Curie treated an estimated one million soldiers using her X-ray devices while acting as the Red Cross Radiology Service director. She went around Paris looking for money, supplies, and conversion cars.

Marie Curie began producing hollow needles containing "radium emanation," a colorless, radioactive gas emitted by radium, in 1915 for use in sterilizing diseased tissue. This gas was later identified as radon. She supplied the radium with a one-gram quantity of her own.

According to estimates, over a million wounded soldiers were treated using her X-ray equipment. She did virtually little scientific research because she was so preoccupied with her career.

She attempted to contribute her gold Nobel Prize medals to the war effort shortly after the war began, but the French National

Bank refused to accept them. She did, however, invest her Nobel Prize money in war bonds.

In France and Belgium, she constructed 200 permanent x-ray stations Over four years, Curie assisted surgeons in locating and removing shrapnel and bullets from the bodies of wounded soldiers by equipping and operating more than twenty ambulances and hundreds of field hospitals with simple x-ray machines.

She not only directly trained and supervised young women in the use of the equipment, but she also drove and operated one herself, despite the dangers of getting too close to the front lines of battle.

After the war, her daughter Irene worked as an assistant at Marie Curie's laboratory. The Curie Foundation was founded in 1920 to research radium's medical applications.Marie Curie was elected to the newly formed International Committee on Intellectual Cooperation of the League of Nations in August 1922. She served on the commission until 1934, contributing to the scientific coordination of the League of Nations alongside other notable scholars such as Albert Einstein, Hendrik Lorentz, and Henri Bergson.

Throughout her life, Curie advocated for the use of radium to alleviate suffering. During World War I, she devoted herself to this cause with the support of her daughter, Irene.

Her interest in science remained throughout her life, and she was instrumental in establishing a radiation laboratory in her hometown. President Herbert Hoover of the United States granted her a $ 50,000 donation from American science friends in 1929 to help her buy radium for her Warsaw laboratory.

Radium and polonium were discovered and used in all sectors of life and medicine at a quick and uncontrollable rate. However, a lack of appropriate dosimetric techniques and safety safeguards led to many major issues; this was something Marie Sklodowska-Curie had intimate experience with. As a result of gaining experience with side effects, modern radiation principles and safety procedures were developed. Radiation is a critical therapeutic strategy in today's oncology.

After studying radiology, anatomy, and automobile mechanics, she built X-ray equipment, cars, auxiliary generators, and mobile radiography units known as Petites Curies or Little Curies.

She progressed through the Red Cross Radiology Service ranks and created France's first military radiology center in late 1914.

They worked at casualty clearing stations near the front lines, X-raying wounded men for fractures, bullets, and shrapnel, at first with the help of a military doctor and her 17-year-old daughter Irène.

Curie coordinated the deployment of 20 mobile radiological vehicles and 200 radiological units on the battlefield during the first year of the war.

In 1895, X-Rays were discovered by Wilhelm Roentgen, but the X-Ray apparatus used to heal the wounded had a limitation. Only in hospitals far from the conflict were they discovered. Her work resulted in the creation of Petites Curie, or mobile radiological equipment.

To overcome the challenge of delivering power, Curie developed a dynamo in the mobile automobile to make and provide the required electricity.

Marie Curie's technology is analogous to that used now in fluoroscopy devices in hospitals, which are advanced X-ray scanners that allow doctors to observe moving images in the body, such as the heart's pumping action or swallowing motion. Curie's study was crucial in the development of contemporary surgical x-rays.

She was named head of the International Red Cross's radiological service, where she trained medical personnel and doctors on how to operate and use the x-ray equipment.She later went on to train other women to be aides.

During the war, Curie equipped and operated more than twenty ambulances and hundreds of field hospitals with rudimentary x-ray machines, assisting medics in detecting and removing shrapnel and bullets from the bodies of wounded soldiers.

Despite the perils of being so near to the front lines of battle, she not only educated and supervised young women in the operation of the equipment, but she also drove and operated one herself. She and her daughter Irene worked in a Casualty Clearing Station, where she assisted in detecting gunshots, fractured bones, and other inside injuries using X-Ray machines.

In the first year of the conflict, she coordinated the installation of 20 mobile radiology vans and 200 radiology units at field hospitals. She also trained 150 women to be X-Ray assistants. By the end of the war, Curie's x-ray equipment and Radon gas syringes, which she devised to sterilize wounds, were thought to have saved a million soldiers.

While serving as the Red Cross Radiology Service director, Curie treated an estimated one million soldiers with her X-ray machines. She scoured Paris for cash, materials, and conversion vehicles.

In 1915, Marie Curie started manufacturing hollow needles containing "radium emanation," a colorless, radioactive gas released by radium, to sterilize sick tissue. This gas was eventually discovered to be radon.

She gave the radium a one-gram dose of her radium. According to estimates, over a million wounded soldiers were treated with her X-ray equipment. Because she was so consumed with her profession, she did very little scientific research.

Shortly after the war began, she attempted to donate her gold Nobel Prize medals to the war effort, but the French National Bank refused to accept them. On the other hand, her Nobel Prize money was invested in war bonds.

Marie Curie chose to contribute even more to the French military effort. She put her prize money into war bonds and outfitted ambulances with medical-grade portable x-ray devices. She built 200 permanent x-ray stations in France and Belgium.

Over four years, Curie equipped and operated more than twenty ambulances and hundreds of field hospitals with rudimentary x-ray machines, assisting surgeons in finding and extracting shrapnel and bullets from the bodies of wounded soldiers.

Despite the perils of being too near to the front lines of battle, she not only educated and supervised young women in the operation of the equipment, but she also drove and operated one herself.

Irene, her daughter, worked as an assistant at Marie Curie's laboratory after the war. The Curie Foundation was established in 1920 to study the medical applications of radium.

In August 1922, Marie Curie was chosen to the League of Nations newly founded International Committee on Intellectual Cooperation. She remained on the commission until 1934, contributing to the League of Nations' scientific cooperation alongside Albert Einstein, Hendrik Lorentz, and Henri Bergson, among others.